The Official RANGERS Annual 2010

Written by Douglas Russell

A Grange Publication

© 2009. Published by Grange Communications Ltd., Edinburgh, under licence from Rangers Football Club. Printed in the EU.

Photographs © Rangers Football Club & SNS Group.

ISBN 978-1-906211-87-5

£6.99

CONTENTS

A CHAMPIONSHIP SEASON

THE 2008/09 SPL CAMPAIGN

AUGUST

Rangers travelled to Falkirk in what proved to be a hard-fought opening day SPL fixture. Allan McGregor was the hero when he saved a Higdon penalty and that was the turning point as summer signing Andrius Velicka bagged the only goal with a close-range finish following good work from fellow new boy Kyle Lafferty and Kris Boyd.

Against Hearts at Ibrox, Kyle Lafferty struck his first goal for the Light Blues with a crisp shot from Madjid Bougherra's low pass and Kris Boyd sealed the points late on with a thunderous penalty past McDonald after Kenny Miller had been brought down in the area. Pedro Mendes (a Champions League winner with Porto)

oozed class throughout the ninety minutes and the playmaker from Portugal was deservedly named Man of the Match on his Rangers debut.

Three points should have been secured at Pittodrie in the clash with Aberdeen when substitute DaMarcus Beasley rifled home at the end of the game but the goal was wrongly disallowed for offside. Earlier, Rangers had taken a deserved lead when David Weir met Kevin Thomson's accurate free kick and headed past Langfield in goal. In added time before the break, however, the home side equalised when the ball fell kindly for Young after Allan McGregor's reflex save from a close range Miller header. Rangers should have

left Pittodrie with maximum points as TV replays later proved Beasley's goal was legitimate.

Kenny Miller was the hero for Rangers in the first Old Firm derby of the 2008/09 campaign as the Scotland star struck twice against former club Celtic in a stunning 4-2 victory at Parkhead. Daniel Cousin – in his last game before joining English Premiership newcomers Hull City – opened the scoring with a tremendous goal. After brushing aside defender Wilson with relative ease, the Gabon international cut in from the right and smashed a low shot from a tight angle past Boruc. Samaras equalised within two minutes but Walter Smith's side really began to pull the strings in the second half and Kenny Miller restored Rangers lead with a terrific volley. Then, from a corner, Steven Davis played the ball back to Pedro Mendes (SPL Player of the Month) and the maestro hit a venomous strike from 25 yards that flashed past the Celtic keeper. Kenny Miller later claimed his second of the game when a Boruc error allowed the alert striker to roll home from close range. Nakamura hit a late consolation but there was no doubt that this was a wonderfully impressive away win for the Light Blues. The last visiting side to net four goals against Celtic at Parkhead was also Rangers - back on New Year's Day, 1994.

SEPTEMBER

Kilmarnock arrived at Ibrox unbeaten with three wins, one draw and no goals conceded from their first four SPL fixtures of the campaign. Jim Jefferies' men were obviously intent on continuing this fine start and took an early lead (courtesy of defender Wright) in the first half. After the break, it was Kris Boyd to the rescue and his brace – a penalty after substitute Nacho Novo had been fouled followed by a finish from close range – secured another victory for Rangers. Boyd had now scored 11 goals in 10 games against his former club since his switch up the M77 in January 2006.

Kenny Miller was the architect of both goals in the 2-1 home win over Motherwell. Rangers took the lead early in the second period when his precise through-ball was clinically despatched past Smith by Steven Davis for the Northern Irishman's first goal since agreeing a permanent Ibrox deal. Ten minutes later, Miller's superb driven cross from the right was bundled home by Nacho Novo whose second half substitute appearance had paid dividends in consecutive games. Clarkson scored a consolation for Motherwell but the Light Blues held firm for another 2-1 triumph. Rangers had now won every home league match since the October 2007 win over Celtic – a total of 17 SPL games.

After netting a double against one of his former clubs in August, Kenny Miller claimed another brace in the Easter Road clash with previous employers Hibernian. His first was a low diving header from Kirk Broadfoot's delivery into the penalty area. Then he finished a clever move involving both Mendes and Broadfoot with a clinical left foot strike that curled past a helpless Ma-Kalambay in goal. Defender Madjid Bougherra completed a fine afternoon's work in the capital when he bundled home the third from Kevin Thomson's lofted free-kick into the box.

OCTOBER

Despite languishing at the foot of the league table, St Mirren upset the odds to take all three points at Love Street and record their first home win over Rangers since April 1986. Incidentally, back then, Walter Smith was only days into his new Ibrox job as Assistant to Graeme Souness. The only goal of the October 2008 game – and indeed St Mirren's solitary shot on target – was scored by substitute Stephen McGinn (grandson of former Celtic chairman Jack McGinn) deep into the second period. After that, a Boyd header hit the post and both Lafferty and Broadfoot came close but not close enough for Rangers, who were now on the same points total as Celtic in the Championship race.

Following the international break for World Cup qualifying games, the SPL fixture against Dundee United was postponed due to the sad death of their club chairman Eddie Thompson. Away to Hamilton Academical at New Douglas Park in dreadfully wet and windy conditions, Kris Boyd netted either side of half time - the first was from the penalty spot - after Easton had given Billy Reid's side an early lead. Substitute Nacho Novo, after a prolonged period of Rangers domination, then made it 3-1 with a neat finish near the end of the game.

NOVEMBER

The side's next league clash was their first home SPL game since the visit of Motherwell in late September. With Kenny Miller and Kris Boyd continuing their striking partnership, Rangers were on fire right from the start and destroyed Inverness Caledonian Thistle with a first half blitz of five goals. Nacho Novo opened the scoring after keeper Fraser failed to hold a powerful Boyd strike from 22 yards. Boyd himself then netted twice before a converted penalty confirmed a well-deserved hat trick for the predatory finisher.

The pick of that afternoon's goals, however, was number five when Kenny Miller hit a ferocious volley high into the net following Novo's lofted ball into the heart of the area.

On a night of high drama at Ibrox, Dundee United - six wins and a draw from their last seven games - came close to securing all three points after taking the lead twice in an enthralling 3-3 draw. Steven Davis opened the scoring early on with a right foot strike into the bottom corner of the net. After equalising through Sandaza, the visitors gained the advantage when the Spaniard claimed his second. Then, just before the break, Sasa Papac scored his first ever Rangers goal with an unstoppable left foot strike after surging into the box. Craig Levein's side made it 3-2 courtesy of Robertson in the second period and that's how it remained until the second minute of added time when Kevin Thomson hit home from the edge of the area, preserving an unbeaten 25-match home record for Walter Smith's men.

Rangers returned to winning ways with a comprehensive 4-0 triumph over Kilmarnock at Rugby Park. Defender David Weir set the ball rolling when he headed past Combe from a set-piece at the start of the second period. Kris Boyd, who had missed a first half penalty, then thumped home from a glorious arched Kenny Miller pass before provider became scorer with a headed goal. Substitute Steven Whittaker netted number four right at the end to seal a convincing victory in Ayrshire. Sadly post-match joy was short-lived when it was confirmed that the injury suffered by Kevin Thomson during the game would keep the influential midfielder out of action for the remainder of the season.

Creating opportunities to score was not a problem in the game with Motherwell at Fir Park but converting those chances proved to be another matter. When Rangers did eventually have the ball in the net (in the second period, thanks to an onside Kris Boyd) a linesman's error cost Rangers victory yet again. As Walter Smith correctly pointed out after the 0-0 result, this was the second time this season that his side had dropped points due to a crucial mistake by a referee's assistant.

Rangers took command of the home clash with St Mirren from the whistle and Kris Boyd and Steven Davis fired the Light Blues into an early lead. Argentine full back Miranda netted late on to make it 2-1 then Allan McGregor produced a terrific save from Dargo's free kick right at the end to secure another victory for Walter Smith's men.

With first team regulars Kenny Miller, Madjid Bougherra, Steven Davis and Sasa Papac all missing the SPL clash with Aberdeen, Jean-Claude Darcheville partnered Kris Boyd in attack and Lee McCulloch was deployed as a central defender alongside David Weir. French frontman Darcheville broke the deadlock for Rangers when he stabbed home from close range and the prolific Boyd sealed a 2-0 win which kept the side on Celtic's tail in the race for the league title. Charlie Adam created both goals from corners in the game that marked the 20th anniversary of Sir David Murray's tenure at Rangers.

Major disappointment followed at Tynecastle as poor defending at set pieces cost Smith's men the loss of two early goals. Even though a Karipidis own goal reduced the deficit to 2-1 before the break, Rangers could not force an equaliser against Hearts in the second period.

It was back to winning ways the following week on a day when Kris Boyd claimed the 7th hat-trick of his Ibrox career. Rangers, firing on all cylinders, demolished visitors Hamilton Academical 7-1. First half strikes from Kenny Miller and Boyd – after Accies had taken a second-minute lead – were followed by goals in the second period from Boyd (2), Kyle Lafferty, Nacho Novo and Steven Davis. Certainly the dismissal of Canning when he conceded a 50th minute penalty to Boyd did little to help the visitors' cause but, nevertheless, it was still a fine performance by Rangers with the returning duo of Miller and Davis particularly impressive.

With the statistics confirming only one win in the previous eight SPL trips to Tannadice – a 4-1 victory in April 2006 - the away clash against Dundee United was obviously fraught with danger. However, Rangers began the game with real purpose and Kris Boyd opened the scoring early on with a superb finish. Steven Whittaker's delivery from the right was cleverly dummied by Steven Davis before Boyd, after turning defender Wilkie, lashed a left-foot drive past Zaluska from the edge of the box. Despite dominating the remainder of the first period, the Light Blues failed to add to their tally. Then, right at the start of the second half, failure to deal with routine crosses into the box resulted in the loss of two goals and the game was turned on its head. With fifteen minutes remaining, substitutes Nacho Novo and Kyle Lafferty combined effectively for the Northern Ireland striker to equalise with a classy side foot finish that ensured a 2-2 draw.

Hibernian – the last team to win at Ibrox in SPL action – arrived in Glasgow on the back of a five-game unbeaten run that included an impressive 2-0 home victory over league leaders Celtic earlier in the month. With two well-organised banks of four, Mixu Paatelainen's side defended impressively, restricting the Light Blues to very few genuine chances. In the second half, however, a really special goal won the game for Rangers. Following a Steven Davis corner from the right, Kris Boyd, with his back to goal, delivered an acrobatic, diagonal overhead kick from ten yards that found the bottom corner of Ma-Kalambay's net. Pedro Mendes then nearly stole the striker's thunder with an audacious soaring shot from all of forty yards that rose and dipped before crashing off the bar with the Hibernian keeper beaten.

The final Old Firm clash of 2008 was decided by Scott McDonald's second half strike and confirmed Celtic's first Ibrox victory in almost three years. Earlier in the game, Rangers could have taken the lead when a superb Barry Ferguson pass put Kris Boyd through on Boruc but the big keeper got his body behind the shot and saved well.

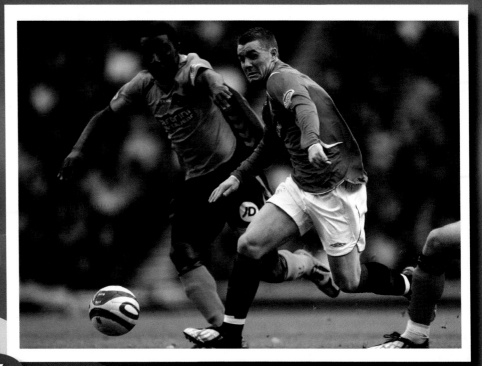

JANUARY

Rangers recovered from the Old Firm defeat at Inverness Caledonian Thistle in the New Year. A sublime goal from Pedro Mendes settled any nerves and what a strike it was! The midfielder from Portugal curled a quite breathtaking strike from all of 25 yards into the top corner beyond keeper Eason following a fine Rangers breakaway. The Light Blues then took control for the remainder of the game and Kris Boyd netted twice in the last eight minutes, taking his season's SPL tally to 18.

Another brace from Boyd was a key factor in the 3-1 win over Falkirk at Ibrox. Although Lovell had opened the scoring for the visitors, Rangers drew level thanks to a Kris Boyd penalty right at the close of the first half. Ten minutes before the end of the game, the striker was once again in the right place to touch home after keeper Olejnik failed to hold a low drive from the right by substitute Nacho Novo. Incidentally, both teams were down to ten men by this stage following the harsh dismissals of Cregg and Sasa Papac. Then, just before the final whistle, a delightful solo effort from Steven Davis was the icing on the cake. Man of the Match was 17 year old John Fleck who made his first SPL start and completed the ninety minutes on the left side of midfield. Kris Boyd, for the record, had now scored almost 40% of the Club's 51 league goals to date.

Pittodrie has proved to be a difficult venue in the recent past. Indeed the last win for Rangers in the Granite City was back in December 2006 before Walter Smith's return to the Club. Aberdeen, riding high after six consecutive home wins including an impressive 4-2 victory over Celtic the previous week, faced a more containing 4-5-1 Rangers formation with Kenny Miller starting as lone striker and Kris Boyd on the bench. Although openings were limited for either side, the visitors created some good chances late-on following the introduction of both Boyd and Novo but the contest eventually ended in a 0-0 stalemate.

On the last day of January, Dundee United (defending an unbeaten league record against the Old Firm this season) again offered stern resistance and it was into the final fifteen minutes before Rangers gained the upper hand. Youngster John Fleck, in his third start for Smith's side, was bundled off the ball in the area before picking himself up and calmly steering the resultant penalty past Zaluska. It was his first senior goal for the Club. Gaps then started to appear as the visitors pushed for an equaliser and, just before the final whistle, substitute Kyle Lafferty wrapped up the points with a left foot finish and his side's 31st home goal of the SPL campaign.

FEBRUARY

The third Old Firm derby of the season ended 0-0 as Rangers earned a fighting point against Celtic at Parkhead. Rangers created the better of the chances in the second period but neither side could break the deadlock and Rangers remained two points behind in the title race.

Kenny Miller, after his double against Forfar in the Homecoming Scottish Cup earlier in the week, made it four in four days with a brace in the 3-1 win over Kilmarnock. The visitors took an early lead courtesy of Hamill but Kris Boyd soon cancelled out that advantage when Madjid Bougherra nodded down a Pedro Mendes corner and the striker rifled home for his 21st goal in 23 league outings. Miller's goals (two in three minutes, also in the first half) were both beautifully executed – the first, a left foot drive and the second, a delightful finish past Combe with the outside of his right boot. Rangers now headed the Scottish Premier League for the first time since November 1.

At New Douglas Park, Rangers held their ground at the top of the table following a tight 1-0 win over Hamilton Academical. Barry Ferguson netted the winner (his first goal of the campaign) late in the first half when a left foot snap-shot from the edge of the area found the bottom corner of the net through a crowd of players. This was the first time that keeper Cerny had lost a goal at home since the end of November. With Pedro Mendes missing, Maurice Edu had the chance to shine in the middle of the park, following an early injury to Lee McCulloch - and the young American impressed alongside Ferguson as Hamilton Academical's previous unbeaten run of six games came to an end.

MARCH

Bottom of the league Inverness Caledonian Thistle (now managed by Rangers legend Terry Butcher) arrived in Glasgow for the first mid week league fixture at Ibrox since November. Despite having the bulk of possession for virtually all of the game, Smith's men failed to breach the visitors' well-organised defence and, right at the end, were made to suffer when Black netted from the spot. This penalty followed some indecision at the back and David Weir was red-carded for a foul on Proctor. With Celtic winning at Rugby Park, Rangers greatest rivals now held a three point advantage as league leaders.

Then, following two weeks of domestic cup action, Rangers returned to SPL duty for the visit of third place Hearts. Despite the absence of defenders Broadfoot, Bougherra and Weir, first half goals from Kyle Lafferty (an emphatic low drive from the right side of the area) and Barry Ferguson (a powerful shot across the keeper into the far corner) seemed to set the team on the road to a convincing win. After adopting a 4-4-2 formation for the second period however, Csaba Laszlo's team staged an unlikely comeback and eventually ended the game all-square at 2-2.

At Westfield against Falkirk on the first day of the SPL campaign, Andrius Velicka claimed the only goal of the game. Although the Lithuanian made a late substitute appearance at the same venue the week before Easter, it was fellow striker Kris Boyd who grabbed the headlines this time. With less than ten minutes played, Nacho Novo's low delivery across the box was despatched past Dani Mallo by Boyd. This early advantage – the striker's 25th goal of the season – proved to be decisive as there was no more scoring in the game.

The last time Rangers played St Mirren away, the Paisley outfit recorded a surprising 1-0 win.

At new St Mirren Park, however, early first half goals from Kris Boyd and Maurice Edu (a powerful near-post header from a Pedro Mendes corner) were enough to secure the points after Gus MacPherson's side pulled one back in the second period. St Mirren's goal was, in fact, the first the Rangers defence had conceded away from home in the SPL since the trip to Tannadice in mid-December.

Two goals in the first ten minutes – Andrius Velicka steered home from close range before Kris Boyd struck with a quite astonishing angled half-volley from 25 yards – set the pulses racing against Motherwell at Ibrox. Although Mark McGhee's side scored before the break, Kris Boyd converted a second half penalty to secure a 3-1 win. This was Rangers third SPL game (and victory) in six days.

The final encounter before the league split was a capital clash with Hibernian at Easter Road. On a gloriously sunny Sunday afternoon, the fans had barely settled in their seats when Steven Whittaker netted against his former club with a wonderful dipping volley from distance. Although Fletcher equalised before the break, Andrius Velicka restored Rangers advantage with a stunning right foot strike from a tight angle before Maurice Edu made it 3-1 from a close range effort. A second Hibernian goal (Rankin's tremendous strike) ensured drama up until the final whistle but Rangers defended resolutely to seal a terrific win. The last time Rangers won four consecutive SPL matches was back in September and, coincidentally, Hibernian also provided the opposition for the final game of that run.

MAY

Andrius Velicka, with his fourth goal in as many games, opened the scoring against Hearts as the first half drew to a close at Ibrox. On this occasion, Kris Boyd turned provider after his nod down from a Steven Smith corner was fired home by the Lithuanian striker. Boyd then claimed his 30th of the season when he bundled home a driven cross from the right by Kenny Miller. Although Hearts had played and passed well throughout, the Tynecastle side lacked the cutting edge of their opponents in blue. With four games to play, Rangers remained one point behind leaders Celtic in the race for SPL glory.

One week later, Walter Smith's side returned to the top of the SPL table following a 1-0 win in the final Old Firm fixture of the campaign. Ten minutes before the break, Kenny Miller, from Boyd's lay-off, burst into the box past Hinkel and delivered a low cutback across the area that Steven Davis, arriving at speed, met at the back post to bundle past Boruc. It was the midfielder's sixth league goal of the season and Celtic had no response.

Back at Easter Road for the third time this season, Rangers trailed 1-0 at half time after Derek Riordan's goal gave Hibernian an advantage just before the break. Following the substitute appearance of both Kyle Lafferty and Nacho Novo, Rangers began to attack with far more pace and purpose and ten minutes from time Novo bundled home the equaliser. Novo thought he had the ball in the net before that – and TV replays suggested the Spaniard had struck – but the match officials ruled his effort out and Celtic now led the SPL on goal difference.

Controversial red cards for both Charlie Mulgrew and Madjid Bougherra added to the drama when Aberdeen provided the opposition for the last home game of the season. All three points were secured thanks mainly to Kenny Miller's second half contribution. After out-pacing Mair wide left, the striker hit a fast delivery into the box that Foster buried past Langfield for an own goal. Then, just two minutes later, Miller increased the lead with a well-judged header after Nacho Novo's perfect delivery from a corner. Although Paton

subsequently scored for the visitors, Rangers had done enough to take the points.

With Celtic drawing at Easter Road in their penultimate game, victory away to Dundee United on the last day of the league campaign would now secure the SPL title for Walter Smith's side. Despite the last-day pressure, Rangers were in total command from the start and produced a performance of great quality. Kyle Lafferty opened the scoring early on and then, just before the break, a Sasa Papac free-kick rebounded off the defensive wall and Pedro Mendes drilled home through a crowded area. Kris Boyd sealed an impressive 3-0 victory when he met Steven Whittaker's superb right wing cross and the Championship party was well and truly on. The SPL trophy was presented to the Light Blues at the end of the game and over 30,000 loyal supporters returned to Ibrox after the match to welcome their heroes.

Walter Smith had guided Rangers to nine-in-a-row at Tannadice in 1997 but the 2008/09 title success was just as sweet for the supporters and everyone at the Club as Championship number 52 was secured in some style.

THE HOMECOMING
SCOTTISH CUP CAMPAIGN 2009

Rangers joined the 2008/09 Homecoming Scottish Cup at the fourth round stage of the competition. The first obstacle on the road to retaining the trophy was a difficult away tie at McDiarmid Park, home of Division One leaders (champions in due course) St Johnstone. At the semi final stage of the same tournament the previous season, the Perth side pushed Rangers all the way at Hampden before eventually losing after a penalty shoot-out. This time, the team managed by former Rangers player Derek McInnes dominated from the start and it was only a series of fine stops by Allan McGregor that denied the home side. Just before half-time, however, Rangers opened the scoring when Kris Boyd's low driven cross from the right was converted by defender McCaffrey for an own goal. Smith's men moved up a gear in the second period although the tie was still very open before substitute Nacho Novo made it 2-0 following a lung-bursting run by Steven Davis.

Forfar then lay in wait at Station Park and although Sasa Papac opened the scoring early on, the Third Division side held firm for the remainder of the first period. After the break, however, Kenny Miller doubled the visitors' tally with a fine left foot strike to ensure a smoother passage towards the final whistle. Following the dismissal of Elliot Smith for a dangerous tackle on DaMarcus Beasley, late goals from substitute Aaron Niguez (the young Spaniard's first goal in a Rangers shirt) and Miller (his second of the night) secured a final score of 4-0 and a place for Rangers in the quarter-finals.

Hamilton Academical were the next opponents at Ibrox and the Light Blues secured their place in the last four with a convincing 5-1 win. Steven Whittaker (in for the injured Kirk Broadfoot at right back) opened the scoring with a superb goal – cutting in to the penalty area, he did a 360 degree turn before finding the bottom corner with an accurate left foot strike. Although Quinn then equalised for the visitors, goals from Kyle Lafferty (his sixth for the Club) and Aaron Niguez (a re-taken penalty after keeper Cerny was penalised for moving on his line) gave Rangers a 3-1 advantage at the interval. In the second half, a superb solo effort by Steven Davis and another from Lafferty completed the rout.

Andrius Velicka's goal – with less than two minutes played – was the best possible start for Rangers against St Mirren at Hampden in the semi final of the competition. Although Gus McPherson's side (at this stage of the season the only team to have defeated both sides of the Old Firm) subsequently enjoyed a great deal of possession, Neil Alexander was rarely troubled. In the second half, Kris Boyd hit his 100th goal for the Club with a left foot drive across the keeper following a superb run by Steven Davis. Substitute Kenny Miller completed the scoring with his first goal in two months, again after good play from Davis.

Six days after securing the SPL title at Tannadice, Rangers faced Falkirk at the National Stadium in the final of the Homecoming Scottish Cup. In sweltering conditions, John Hughes' side had the better of the first half and created more goalscoring opportunities than the league Champions. Nacho Novo replaced Kris Boyd at the start of the second period and less than 30 seconds after his introduction the livewire Spaniard crashed an unstoppable volley into the net to secure a stunning double for the Light Blues. Novo's strike earned Rangers their 33rd Scottish Cup triumph and an incredible season ended in joy at Hampden.

WHO SAID THAT LAST SEASON?

1. "I really loved that match. The blood is right under your skin, but you cannot let that get to your head. The pressure is there, but you need to distance yourself from it."

2. "He is a nice lad and his command of the English language is probably better than the majority in the dressing room – including the Scots."

3. "If I am being picky then I thought he should have hit the shot across the keeper."

4. "He showed what he's all about. That took a lot of bottle and he struck it home nicely."

5. "If Kris Boyd had been playing for us, we would have won."

6. "I caught one sweet as a nut last week against Hibs and it hit Sol Bamba on the chest. Today, I didn't catch it as sweet and it went in."

7. "He is a great person and Manager. It's a pleasure to work for him. He is a gentleman and right up there with those in my career."

8. "When the final whistle did eventually sound, I just tore on the pitch. I didn't know where I was running or why I was running. I just ran."

Answers on page 62

HAMPDEN MAY 30, 2009

PLAYER PROFILES

Neil Alexander

Goalkeeper Neil Alexander made his Rangers debut back in February 2008 after Allan McGregor had been sent off towards the end of a Scottish Cup tie with Hibernian at Easter Road. With McGregor unavailable through injury, Edinburgh-born Alexander kept goal for three consecutive winning games in September – the SPL victories over Motherwell (2-1) and Hibernian (3-0), as well as the Co-operative Insurance Cup clash with Partick Thistle at Firhill that ended 2-1 in Rangers favour. Then, towards the end of the 2008/09 campaign, the keeper was recalled for the league encounter with Falkirk at Westfield. Rangers won the game 1-0 and Alexander retained his place for the remainder of the campaign.

Allan McGregor

Following his injury during the April 2008 Old Firm clash at Celtic Park, Allan McGregor missed the remainder of that season including both the final of the UEFA Cup and the Scottish Cup. He was back between the sticks for the start of the 2008/09 campaign and proved his worth with a penalty save away to Falkirk in the opening SPL game. After missing three games in September, McGregor was a constant in Walter Smith's side for a run of 28 domestic league and cup games – 17 wins, 6 draws and 5 defeats - from the beginning of October until the end of March. He lost his place to Alexander near the end of the campaign but McGregor remains one of the best shot-stoppers in the Scottish game.

Steven Whittaker

Last season, his second in Glasgow after signing from Hibernian, Steven Whittaker began to thrive as a Rangers player, filling both full back positions to maximum effect as and when required. Towards the end of the season on the road to Championship glory, he was simply outstanding. Although he scored in the 4-0 win over Kilmarnock at Rugby Park in November after a substitute appearance from the bench, it was his other league goal (at Easter Road in April) that really made the headlines – a quite astonishing half-volley from distance against his former club. Steven was arguably one of the best players in the remaining weeks of the double winning campaign and deserved to collect SPL and Scottish Cup medals.

Sasa Papac

Injury at an important late stage of the season meant that Sasa Papac also missed crucial games in the Championship run-in but, unlike Broadfoot, he was back in action before the end and made the starting line-up for the last home game of the season against Aberdeen. One week later at Tannadice, he was quite exceptional. The quietly confident Papac had enjoyed a wonderfully impressive campaign at left back, beginning a total of 36 games for the men in blue. His first-ever goal for Rangers was during the thrilling 3-3 draw at Ibrox with Dundee United when he ended a surging run into the box with a fine left foot strike past Celtic-bound Zaluska. Papac, a consistent performer, also netted away to Forfar at Station Park in the 4-0 Homecoming Scottish Cup win.

David Weir

David Weir began his professional career with Falkirk before joining Hearts in 1996 where he won the 1998 Scottish Cup. Then, in 1999, the defender moved south to Everton where he became club captain under two different managers, Walter Smith and David Moyes. It was Walter Smith, of course, who subsequently brought the player to Ibrox in January 2007. Throughout the various domestic and European campaigns of Season 2007/08, Weir was immense as Rangers secured both domestic cups as well as coming close to winning not only the league championship but also the UEFA Cup. Last term, in his second full season with the Club, the veteran started more games than any other first team player and ended the campaign as Club Captain, famously lifting both the SPL trophy and the Homecoming Scottish Cup at Tannadice and Hampden respectively.

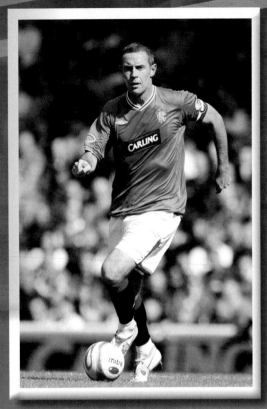

Madjid Bougherra

Madjid Bougherra, a bargain buy from Charlton last summer, was so impressive throughout his debut season in Scotland he was voted Rangers Player of the Year by the fans. Blessed with pace, power and a great touch, he was a tower of strength in a number of important games throughout the campaign. Madjid forged a formidable partnership with David Weir at the heart of the Rangers defence and was Man of the Match on Homecoming Scottish Cup final day at Hampden in May 2009 as Rangers secured a fantastic double.

Kevin Thomson

Midfielder Kevin Thomson began the 2008/09 campaign as he had ended the previous one – in superb form. The player was virtually an ever-present in the side until being seriously injured at Rugby Park in November towards the end of the 4-0 SPL win over Kilmarnock. His season now over, it was a devastating blow for both the player and his Club. Thomson's first goal for Rangers was the crucial Old Firm winner against Celtic in March 2008. Last season, he claimed another extremely important strike when he netted right at the end of the enthralling Ibrox clash with Dundee United, making it 3-3 on the night. This late goal (in the second minute of added time) preserved the Club's 25 match unbeaten home record. Just one week later, however, his season ended abruptly with cruciate ligament damage in Ayrshire. Thankfully, after months of rehabilitation and hard work, Thomson has recovered and is ready for action soon after the start of 2009/10.

Steven Davis

The Ballymena born playmaker (Northern Ireland's youngest modern day captain) ended his first full season at Ibrox as the Rangers Players' Player of the Year for Season 2008/09. In addition to his midfield heroics last term, Steven Davis also hit some timely and important goals for Walter Smith's side. His first – the opener in the September 2-1 home win over Motherwell – was followed by another opening goal when Rangers and Dundee United drew 3-3 at Ibrox in early November. Although subsequent SPL strikes against St Mirren, Hamilton Academical, Falkirk and a goal in the 5-1 Homecoming Scottish Cup win over Hamilton Academical were all naturally celebrated, it was his last goal of the 2008/09 campaign that really had the fans singing. That, of course, was the winning strike in the early May Old Firm clash when Rangers beat Celtic 1-0 to regain top spot in the league table. It is worth bearing in mind that Davis is only 24 years old.

Rangers made the following football headlines last season. What was the occasion?

1. Friend Turned Deadly Foe
Daily Mail, 15.9.08

2. The Mend Of The Line
Daily Record, 25.9.08

3. Banishing The Pain
Daily Mail, 28.1.09

4. Edu Provides A Wind Of Change
Daily Mail, 9.4.09

5. It's Deja Blue For Smith
Daily Mail, 15.9.08

6. Ibrox Men Seize The Day And The Title
Glasgow Herald, 25.5.09

7. Big Hand For A Small Wonder
Daily Mail, 1.6.09

ANSWERS ON P63

SEASON 2008/09 QUIZ

1 Who scored Rangers first and last goals of the league campaign?

2 His first award after joining Rangers was SPL Player of the Month for August 2008.

3 What landmark did Kris Boyd reach in the April Homecoming Scottish Cup semi final win over St Mirren at Hampden?

4 Five players made over 30 league starts in 2008/09. Can you name them?

5 This player was capped for his country last season before playing a first team game for Rangers.

6 Excluding Old Firm games, Rangers biggest Ibrox crowd was 50,310. Can you name the visitors that day?

7 This player claimed his first-ever Rangers goal against Dundee United in November.

8 Rangers starting eleven at Tannadice on Championship day included two players without a yellow card to their name. Who were they?

9 Who was top scorer in the games against Celtic?

10 How long had Nacho Novo been on the park at Hampden on Scottish Cup final day when he scored?

ANSWERS ON P63

PLAYER PROFILES

Pedro Mendes

Portuguese midfielder Pedro Mendes joined Rangers on a three-year deal at the start of last season after spells with both Tottenham Hotspur and Portsmouth in the English Premiership. A Champions League winner with Porto in 2004, the player also won an FA Cup medal when Portsmouth beat Cardiff City in the 2008 final at Wembley. From his debut, Mendes impressed in Scotland and was named Man of the Match for his display against Hearts at Ibrox. Then, two weeks later, he scored one of the goals of the season when his stunning strike from distance against Celtic helped Rangers on their way to an unforgettable 4-2 win. Pedro also struck gems against Partick Thistle in the Co-operative Insurance Cup and Inverness Caledonian Thistle in the league but his volley against Dundee United was crucial as he helped Rangers win the SPL title at Tannadice.

Maurice Edu

Born in California in 1986, midfielder Maurice Edu made his Major League Soccer debut for Toronto FC in 2007. At the end of that campaign he was named Rookie of the Year — an award voted for by fellow players, coaches, general managers and reporters from the MLS. The player subsequently agreed a five-year contract with Rangers in the summer of 2008 and wore the colours for the first time when Kilmarnock visited on SPL duty in September. The young American had to wait for his chance in the side but he was fantastic in the latter stages of the campaign and his all-action style makes him a real favourite with supporters. Edu's two goals for Rangers last term came in April and proved to be the decisive winning strikes in SPL games with St Mirren (2-1) and Hibernian (3-2), both away from home.

Steven Naismith

Highly rated by everyone at Rangers, the young Scot is equally at home as a striker or on the left side of midfield. Naismith began his senior career at Kilmarnock where he was named Scottish Football Writers' Young Player of the Year for Season 2005/06. At the end of the following campaign (2006/07), he collected another Young Player of the Year award but this time it was from the PFA, his fellow professionals. Naismith arrived at Ibrox on the August 2007 transfer deadline day and made his Rangers debut less than 24 hours later when he appeared as a substitute late on, to great acclaim, during the SPL home game with Gretna. His first goal for the Club was in the 3-0 win over Aberdeen in September 2007. Luck certainly deserted the player later that season and he was seriously injured during the Scottish Cup semi final win over St Johnstone at Hampden. Coincidentally, it was against the same team in the same competition that Naismith returned to first team action in January 2009.

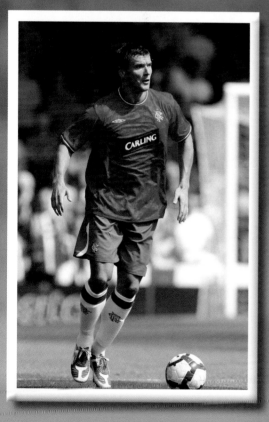

Lee McCulloch

After joining Rangers from Wigan for the start of Season 2007/08, Lee McCulloch scored on his debut against FK Zeta in the Champions League qualifying round. The player ended the campaign having made 38 starts with seven goals in all competitions — three in the SPL, two in the Scottish Cup and two in the Champions League. Indeed his superb goal at the Stade Gerland in France against Lyon in the latter competition was one of the highlights of the season. Sadly his second year at Ibrox was blighted with a series of injuries and the versatile McCulloch was limited to just 14 starting appearances for Walter Smith's title winning side. His final start for Rangers in the 2008/09 SPL campaign was the crucial 2-0 home win against Hearts at the beginning of May.

Nacho Novo

Nacho Novo celebrated as much as anyone at Tannadice in May and the image of the player hoisting Walter Smith aloft at the final whistle was an enduring one. Six days later, the Manager would surely have returned the compliment following the Spaniard's wonder goal in the Scottish Cup final. During Season 2008/09, Novo made more substitute appearances for the Club than any other player – a grand total of 28. Indeed, six of his nine campaign goals were scored after he joined the fray from the bench and on both the first and last of those occasions (the 2-1 defeat of Motherwell at Ibrox in September and the Scottish Cup final) he grabbed the winner. Nacho - who has a special rapport with the Ibrox faithful - also netted against Hamilton Academical, Inverness Caledonian Thistle and Hibernian in the SPL, Falkirk in the Co-operative Insurance Cup and St Johnstone in round four of the Homecoming Scottish Cup last season.

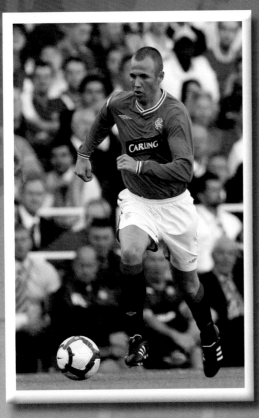

Kenny Miller

Scotland star Kenny Miller played a major role in last season's Double-winning campaign. Early on in 2008/09, his sensational double at Celtic Park in the 4-2 win was followed by another brace against former club Hibs at Easter Road. A league tally of 10 goals was respectable but Miller's tireless contribution to the side is just as important as his strike rate, and his pace and powerful running helped create goals galore for his team-mates. Hampered by a leg nerve complaint for much of the latter part of the 2008/09 campaign, Miller missed the penultimate SPL away game at Hibs but was back in action for the last home match when he created one goal and scored another in the crucial 2-1 win over Aberdeen.

Kris Boyd

Kris Boyd's supreme goal scoring capabilities were evident once again in 2008/09 as the prolific marksman blasted 31 goals in all competitions as Rangers won the SPL and Homecoming Scottish Cup Double. His 27 league goals included hat-tricks against Inverness Caledonian Thistle and Hamilton Academical and doubles against Kilmarnock, Hamilton Academical, Inverness, Falkirk and Motherwell and his partnership with Kenny Miller was crucial throughout the campaign. His busy performance on the final day of the SPL season was rewarded with a goal as the Light Blues turned in a classy display to win their 52nd league title and Boyd's contribution throughout the campaign should not be underestimated.

Kyle Lafferty

Following his SPL debut for Rangers away to Falkirk on the opening league game of the season, young Northern Irishman Kyle Lafferty scored his first goal for the Club a week later in the 2-0 SPL win over Hearts at Ibrox. Signed as a striker, the former Burnley star played for much of the campaign on the left side of midfield but he still chipped in with a number of vital goals – not least on the day the Club won the SPL Championship at Dundee Utd. Sadly, the boyhood Rangers fan had to endure a number of niggling and frustrating injuries for much of the 2008/09 campaign but he still played an important part in the SPL and Homecoming Scottish Cup Double.

1894 Rangers 3 Celtic 1 The Club's first-ever Scottish Cup was secured thanks to goals in the
(February) final from Hugh McCreadie, John Barker and John McPherson.

1897 Rangers 5 Dumbarton 1 Rangers became known as 'The 3 Cup Team' after the trophy
joined both the Glasgow and Charity Cups at Ibrox.

1898 Rangers 2 Kilmarnock 0 On the day of the final, R.C. Hamilton not only scored at
Hampden but also sat a morning exam at Glasgow University!

1903 Rangers 1 Hearts 1
Rangers 0 Hearts 0 (Replay)
Rangers 2 Hearts 0 (Replay) After two drawn games against Hearts, gate prices were
halved to sixpence (2.5p) for the second replay.

1928 Rangers 4 Celtic 0 A quarter of a century later, the trophy eventually returned to Ibrox
following a famous final when cup holders Celtic were humbled 4-0.

1930 Rangers 0 Partick Thistle 0
Rangers 2 Partick Thistle 1 (Replay) This win was part of a grand slam that included
League Championship, Glasgow Cup and Charity Cup.

1932 Rangers 1 Kilmarnock 1
Rangers 3 Kilmarnock 0 (Replay) The Club's 7th Scottish Cup win was courtesy of
goals from Jimmy Fleming, Bob McPhail and Sammy English in the final.

1934 Rangers 5 St Mirren 0 Billy Nicholson netted twice in a comfortable victory. Earlier
in the tournament, Jimmy Fleming established a Club record with nine goals in the 14-2
win over Blairgowrie.

1935 Rangers 2 Hamilton Academical 1 Another double season – a week earlier, the
Championship had been secured at Pittodrie following a 3-1 win.

1936 Rangers 1 Third Lanark 0 The great Bob McPhail claimed the winner after only ninety
seconds of play.

1948 Rangers 1 Morton 1
Rangers 1 Morton 0 (Replay) Billy Williamson, playing his first cup-tie for Rangers,
headed the crucial goal in extra-time before a huge crowd of over 133,000.

1949 Rangers 4 Clyde 1 Scotland's first-ever domestic treble of League Championship,
League Cup and Scottish Cup was won this season.

1950 Rangers 3 East Fife 0 Willie Thornton scored twice on another memorable Hampden
day for the Ibrox legend.

1953 Rangers 1 Aberdeen 1
Rangers 1 Aberdeen 0 (Replay) A Billy Simpson strike won the day for Struth's men.

1960 Rangers 2 Kilmarnock 0 Jimmy Millar's double confirmed Rangers 15th Scottish Cup.

1962 Rangers 2 St Mirren 0 Ralph Brand and Davie Wilson formed a formidable left wing
partnership in the 1960s. Both players scored on cup final day.

1963   Rangers 1 Celtic 1

Rangers 3 Celtic 0 (Replay)   Midfielder Jim Baxter was magnificent as Rangers crushed Celtic in the first Old Firm final for 35 years.

1964   Rangers 3 Dundee 1   Ralph Brand became the first player to score in three successive Scottish Cup finals.

1966   Rangers 0 Celtic 0

Rangers 1 Celtic 0   Kai Johansen's wonder strike won the cup for Rangers. The Dane was the first foreign player to receive a Scottish Cup winner's medal.

1973   Rangers 3 Celtic 2   The Centenary Scottish Cup final was won in dramatic fashion by Tom Forsyth's famous goal with the sole of his boot from close range.

1976   Rangers 3 Hearts 1   At the end of another treble season for the Club, centre forward Derek Johnstone claimed a double, taking his season's tally to 31.

1978   Rangers 2 Aberdeen 1   Derek Johnstone scored the winning goal and the Club secured a second treble in just three years.

1979   Rangers 0 Hibernian 0

Rangers 0 Hibernian 0 (Replay)

Rangers 3 Hibernian 2 (Replay)   It was an extra-time own goal by Arthur Duncan in the second replay that eventually decided the destination of the trophy.

1981   Rangers 0 Dundee United 0

Rangers 4 Dundee United 1 (Replay)   With Davie Cooper, John MacDonald and Derek Johnstone reinstated after the 0-0 draw, a rampant Rangers cruised to victory.

1992   Rangers 2 Airdrie 1   Goals from Mark Hateley and Ally McCoist finally ended an 11 year wait.

1993   Rangers 2 Aberdeen 1   Neil Murray, the youngest player on the park, opened the scoring before Hateley added a second.

1996   Rangers 5 Hearts 1   Gordon Durie's hat-trick was the first in a Scottish Cup final since 1972 and only the third in the history of the competition.

1999   Rangers 1 Celtic 0   Rod Wallace's winner was the icing on another treble cake that season.

2000   Rangers 4 Aberdeen 0   The famous 'final of orange' when huge numbers of Rangers fans wore Holland colours as a 'thank you' to Manager Dick Advocaat.

2002   Rangers 3 Celtic 2   In injury time, winger Peter Lovenkrands headed the late winner on one of those really special Hampden days.

2003   Rangers 1 Dundee 0   Lorenzo Amoruso, the first foreign player to captain Rangers to a treble, claimed the only goal of the game at the national stadium.

2008   Rangers 3 Queen of the South 2   Both domestic cups were secured thanks, in no small part, to Kris Boyd who netted twice in the CIS and Scottish Cup finals.

2009   Rangers 1 Falkirk 0   Nacho Novo's astonishing goal right at the start of the second half was enough to lift the cup and ensure a league and cup double for Walter Smith's side.

GOAL OF THE SEASON

Nacho Novo v Falkirk

**Homecoming Scottish Cup final,
Hampden, May 2009**

Collecting a Sasa Papac throw-in wide left, substitute Nacho Novo - on the park for less than a minute – smashed an unstoppable shot towards the Falkirk goal from over 30 yards. His astonishing drive rose, dipped and swerved, leaving a vapour trail in its wake before beating keeper Mallo. Pedro Mendes scored a few crackers throughout the campaign but Nacho's sensational effort was fit to win any final.

IBROX STADIUM

In the late 1880s, Rangers relocated from Kinning Park and the first Ibrox Stadium was constructed on the site now occupied by Edmiston House at the back of the Govan Stand. With a grandstand to accommodate 1200 fans and raised terraces to offer good views, the ground was considered 'state of the art' for its time. The opening fixture on August 20th 1887 against top English club Preston North End was watched by a crowd of 18,000 - even although the estimated capacity was judged to be somewhat lower at 15,000!

In response to the ever-increasing popularity of the sport and to reflect Rangers increasingly dominant position in Scottish football, a superior venue was soon required and, by the turn of the century, another ground (including a grandstand for 4500 and two huge covered enclosures) was built on land right next to that first stadium. Although the capacity rose to 75,000 within two years, the Ibrox Disaster of 1902 meant a rebuild for safety and, subsequently, a reduced limit of 25,000. By 1910, however, Ibrox was a bowl-shaped ground accommodating 63,000 spectators. By the 1920s, the stadium held 80,000.

Central to further development was the construction of the Grandstand (today's Main Stand), officially opened on New Year's Day 1929. In addition to seating for 10,500, there was standing space for thousands more in its enclosures. The imposing red brick façade of the vintage grandstand now enjoys the status of a listed building.

The Ibrox Stadium of today was instigated by the foresight of Manager Willie Waddell in the wake of the 1971 disaster when 66 people died and was given fresh impetus by modern safety legislation and the challenge of meeting the demanding standards of European competition. Three new stands – Copland, Broomloan and Govan – were built during the 1970s and 1980s and a top deck was added to the Main Stand in 1991. The final standing areas were also replaced by seats. Now completely enclosed (with giant screens at two corners), the stadium currently has a capacity of 51,082 following the addition of Bar 72 in 2006.

With computerised ticketing and closed circuit television, Ibrox is one of only 26 football grounds in Europe accorded five-star elite status by UEFA.

MIDFIELD AND MAGNIFICENT

OVER THE YEARS, MANY GIFTED MIDFIELDERS HAVE PLAYED FOR THE CLUB. HERE IS A LOOK AT THE CAREERS OF THREE EXCEPTIONAL PLAYERS WHO SHONE IN THE BLUE OF RANGERS.

Ian Durrant

Ian Durrant, now First Team Coach at the Club, joined his boyhood heroes from school and made his league debut away to Morton in April 1985. By the following season, a blossoming Durrant, now established in the first team, scored on his Old Firm debut when visitors Celtic were comprehensively defeated 3-0.

With the arrival of Graeme Souness as manager, the No 10 jersey would virtually become his own and Ian wore it with pride on no fewer than 39 times that Championship year of 1986/87. The League Cup also returned to the Trophy Room after Durrant's opening goal in the final set Rangers on the road to a 2-1 win over Celtic.

Although the title was not retained in Season 1987/88, the League Cup did remain at Ibrox. Rangers faced Aberdeen at Hampden in October in one of the great finals and it was on this day that the most enduring image of Ian Durrant was captured forever. After the Granite City team opened the scoring, goals from Davie Cooper and Durrant established a Light Blue lead. Aberdeen then netted twice before Robert Fleck claimed a late equaliser and, with no additional scoring in extra-time, it was all down to penalties. Fans of a certain age will never forget that photograph of Durrant, arms high in 'victory v' celebration, after he netted the decisive spot kick.

Following serious injury during a game at Pittodrie in the third month of the 1988/89 campaign, Durrant (whose right knee was virtually shattered in the incident) faced a long spell on the sidelines but when he did return – against Hibernian at Ibrox in April 1991 – 35,000 people rose as one to greet him.

Season 1992/93 was special both home and abroad with a domestic treble and unqualified success in Europe. Durrant netted three times in an unforgettable and unbeaten Champions League campaign – his stunning equaliser against Olympique Marseille in the hostile atmosphere of the Velodrome meant that Rangers became the first visitors in 15 European ties to avoid defeat there. His season ended with the Man of the Match award for a selfless performance in the treble-clinching 1993 Scottish Cup final victory over Aberdeen.

The memories remain many and that abiding image of the player, arms aloft in celebration after scoring, is now part of Ibrox folklore.

Ray Wilkins

Considered one of the finest midfield talents to don the blue of Rangers, Englishman Ray Wilkins joined Rangers in November 1987 having worn the colours of Chelsea, Manchester United and AC Milan. The player had also represented his country no fewer than 84 times.

After his debut against Hearts at Ibrox in November 1987, the playmaker was an ever-present in the team for the rest of that season and claimed his only goal of the campaign in the February 4-0 win over St Mirren. Wilkins endeared himself to the Ibrox legions right from the start by always ushering celebrating players to the crowd after a goal – he knew the true importance of the Club's fan base. The first of his three Scottish medals was acquired that first year when Aberdeen became victims on League Cup final day.

Season 1988/89 had barely started before champions Celtic came calling on a gloriously hot late August afternoon. Very soon Ray Wilkins would score his only league goal of the campaign, very soon Ray Wilkins would be a Ranger for life! Just before the interval, with the game finely balanced at 1-1, the ball dropped to Wilkins at the edge of the Celtic area. Like a predator, he pounced and hit the most perfectly judged right foot volley that screamed past Andrews in goal. Rangers were now ahead and would not be caught. A memorable 5-1 victory was unfolding.

With Razor's assistance, the Championship returned to Ibrox at the end of that campaign - number one of a magnificent nine-in-a-row titles. The League Cup was retained but defeat on Scottish Cup final day (Wilkins missed the game through injury) denied the Club a domestic treble.

He was an ever-present in the league the following season until his last game for Rangers against Dunfermline at Ibrox in late November. Having decided to return home to London for family reasons, Wilkins was given a standing ovation by 40,000 fans as he stood alone in the centre-circle at the end of the game. Ray Wilkins was not the only one to shed a tear that day.

The player's stay in Glasgow may have lasted a mere two years but his name is still held in awe down Ibrox way.

Stuart McCall

Stuart McCall travelled from Liverpool to Glasgow in the summer of 1991, switching the blue of Everton for the blue of Rangers. It was his tenacious, battling midfield qualities that encouraged manager Walter Smith to bring the fiery Scot North in the days when teams could only play a maximum of three 'foreigners' in any European competition.

His first goal for Rangers was against Sparta Prague in the October European Cup tie when he netted twice in the 2-1 win. By season's end, McCall had collected the first of his five League Championship medals with the Club. Then, in October 1992, he claimed the opener against Aberdeen in the Skol Cup final. Rangers triumphed 2-1. The following month at Celtic Park in the 1-0 win, he slotted effortlessly into the right back position as Smith's men progressed towards a domestic treble. The record-breaking Rangers squad of Season 1992/93 had a never-say-die spirit and that summed up McCall.

Week after week in 1994/95, the side had to be changed around mainly due to an unbelievable run of injuries to key players. By early March and the latter stages of the push for seven-in-a-row, the midfielder had become the season's only ever-present in terms of first team appearances.

At the start of the following campaign, his goal against Kilmarnock at Ibrox ensured a successful beginning to the league season. Certainly memorable was his Man of the Match display in the Scottish Cup semi final duel with Celtic in April when he wore the Captain's armband, deputising for the injured Richard Gough. Driving Rangers on to another memorable triumph, he seemed to cover every blade of Hampden grass that day.

He returned to captain Bradford (his first senior club) in the English Premiership for Season 1999/2000 but is still a firm favourite with the Ibrox faithful.

Some footballers develop an affinity with a club's supporters almost immediately. Others never seem to break down that invisible barrier. Stuart McCall rapidly joined the former category – the Ibrox legions realising from the outset that here was a man who would play for the jersey until he dropped. Throughout his Rangers career, he always gave his all.

SUPER GOALS
THE BEST OF SEASON 2008/09

Pedro Mendes
**away v Celtic,
August 2008**

In truth, all four Rangers goals from this SPL win at Celtic Park were rather special but this stunning strike was the pick of the bunch. When Steven Davis cleverly played the ball back to Pedro Mendes from a corner, the playmaker from Portugal unleashed a ferocious drive from distance that found the bottom corner, leaving Boruc flapping.

Kris Boyd
**away v Partick Thistle,
September 2008**

Halfway through the first period of the Co-operative Insurance Cup tie at Firhill, a hopeful lofted pass from Steven Davis descended from the night sky into the penalty area. Kris Boyd watched and waited, following the flight of the ball. Then, without drawing breath, the striker hit a truly unstoppable left-foot volley from an extremely tight angle that soared past Tuffey in goal.

Pedro Mendes
**away v Partick Thistle,
September 2008**

The execution of Rangers winning goal in the same game was simply sensational. Late in extra-time, with a penalty shoot-out fast approaching, substitute DaMarcus Beasley's short pass found Pedro Mendes as the midfielder advanced into the opposition box. Curling a wonderful finish with the outside of his right foot around the Partick Thistle keeper, Mendes then ran to celebrate his astonishing goal with the delirious away support.

Kyle Lafferty
away v Dundee United, December 2008

Despite taking an early lead courtesy of Kris Boyd, Rangers seemed to be heading for defeat after two goals from United turned the game on its head in the second half. Then, with fifteen minutes remaining, Nacho Novo fed fellow substitute Kyle Lafferty who swept the coolest of finishes past Zaluska without breaking stride.

Kenny Miller
home v Inverness Caledonian Thistle, November 2008

Although this game was won at a canter - Rangers destroyed their visitors before the break with five first half goals including a Kris Boyd hat-trick — it was the last goal of the afternoon that really raised the roof at Ibrox. Kenny Miller, after losing his marker, smashed high and home with a tremendous volley following Nacho Novo's floating delivery into the penalty area.

Kris Boyd
home v Hibernian, December 2008

It was going to take something extra special to win this SPL encounter as Hibernian had restricted Rangers with a flexible formation that became a defensive unit of two solid blocks of four players when required. However, on the hour mark following a Davis corner and Broadfoot head flick, Kris Boyd netted the only goal of the game with a spectacular overhead kick in a crowded area.

Pedro Mendes
away v Inverness Caledonian Thistle, January 2009

With memories of his two special strikes against Celtic and Partick Thistle still fresh in the mind, Pedro Mendes completed his very own top three with another gem. This time, at the Caledonian Stadium, he beat the opposition keeper with a bending drive (hit with the inside of his right foot) from 25 yards that winged past Esson into the top corner of the net.

John Fleck
home v Dundee United, January 2009

The youngster's first senior goal for his Club obviously meant a great deal to the player. John Fleck, in only his third start for Walter Smith's side, reached this particular milestone during a SPL clash with Dundee United early in 2009. Late in the game with the score still 0-0, the teenager displayed nerves of steel to score from the penalty spot after being fouled in the box.

Steven Whittaker
home v Hamilton Academical, March 2009

Against Sporting Lisbon in the 2007/08 UEFA Cup campaign, Steven Whittaker scored one of the goals of this season. When Rangers met Hamilton Academical at the quarter-final stage of the Homecoming Scottish Cup in March 2009, the defender opened the scoring with another beauty after cutting into the box from the right and executing a full turn before driving home with a powerful left foot shot.

Kris Boyd
home v Motherwell, April 2009

This was another quite astonishing goal by Kris Boyd. Early in the first period, a Steven Whittaker ball out of defence found the advancing Boyd who, in the blink of an eye, unleashed a venomous angled half-volley from 25 yards that keeper Smith had little chance of saving. A sublime strike with power, pace and direction all judged to perfection.

Steven Whittaker
away v Hibernian, April 2009

Steven Whittaker made his mark with another headline-grabbing strike at the start of the final SPL game before the league split. After controlling a defensive clearance, the Hibernian old boy hit a half-volley from over 20 yards that crashed off the bar and into the back of the net. Steven does not do tap-ins.

Andrius Velicka
away v Hibernian, April 2009

Hibernian keeper Szamotulski really had little chance as Andrius Velicka's blistering drive, from a tight angle, screamed past him to establish a Rangers lead for the second time at Easter Road during the final league game before the top six split.

Kris Boyd
Hampden v St Mirren, April 2009

Although less spectacular than any of his three goals detailed previously in this section, this strike in the semi final of the Homecoming Scottish Cup - a left foot drive across the keeper into the far corner after a strength-sapping run by Steven Davis - is included for one simple reason as it confirmed Kris Boyd's membership of a rather exclusive Ibrox club. The striker had become the 30th player to score 100 goals for Rangers.

Steven Davis
home v Celtic, May 2009

With just four league fixtures remaining and Walter Smith's side one point behind Celtic in the battle for domestic supremacy, this was a must-win game for Rangers. Steven Davis scored the only goal of the derby clash when, cleverly anticipating Kenny Miller's delivery into the box, he timed his back post run to perfection and slid home past Boruc despite the close attention of Maloney.

Kyle Lafferty
away v Dundee United, May 2009

This goal gave Rangers a dream start at Tannadice on the last day of the league season. Steven Davis fed Kris Boyd who then turned his marker inside the box, before squaring for Lafferty to bundle home despite the close attention of his own tangerine shadow. With just six minutes on the clock, it calmed the nerves. Rangers played like real champions for the rest of the game.

The Co-operative Insurance Cup 2008/09

First action in defence of the Co-operative Insurance Cup was a short trip across the Clyde to face Partick Thistle at Firhill. Ian McCall's men had offered stern resistance when the sides met the previous season at the quarter final stage of the Scottish Cup competition and, maybe not surprisingly, a similar scenario again unfolded. Kris Boyd opened the scoring with a quite astonishing left-foot volley that, even at this early stage of the 2008/09 campaign, was a genuine contender for Goal of the Season. After McKeown equalised ten minutes before the break, there was no additional scoring in the ninety minutes, although Rangers had created a whole catalogue of chances. However, deep into extra-time and just four minutes from the lottery of a penalty shoot-out, Pedro Mendes hit the winner, arching a wonderful shot with the outside of his right foot past keeper Tuffey.

Three days after Rangers faced Hamilton Academical on SPL duty, the teams met again at the quarter final stage of this knockout tournament. The Light Blues safely reached the last four following a 2-0 win that was both comfortable and, in truth, rather one-sided. Goals from Kris Boyd (in the first half) and Kyle Lafferty (after the break) ensured another Hampden date following the Club's four successful visits to Scotland's national stadium the previous season. Incidentally, this victory marked Walter Smith's 100th game in charge since his return to Rangers early in 2007.

Against Falkirk at Hampden on semi final night, Allan McGregor was twice called into action early on and denied striker Lovell with good stops. Then, after eight minutes, Nacho Novo opened the scoring when he bundled home from close range following a Pedro Mendes corner. The little Spaniard subsequently claimed his second goal just before the break, finishing well after latching on to a superb ball by Steven Davis. Rangers controlled the bulk of the second period and, right at the end, Kris Boyd completed a good night's work for Smith's men after capitalising on an error by keeper Mallo to make it 3-0.

The final of the competition was an Old Firm affair. This was the first time since Season 2002/03 - when Rangers lifted the CIS Cup after a 2-1 win - that the great rivals had contested a domestic cup final. However, Walter Smith's first ever cup final as a Manager of Rangers facing Celtic ended in disappointment and Gordon Strachan's side lifted the silverware. Although there was little between the teams in the ninety minutes, extra-time goals from O'Dea and McGeady eventually decided the destination of the 2008/09 trophy.

MAN OF THE CENTURY

LAST SEASON, KRIS BOYD BECAME THE FIRST RANGERS PLAYER TO HIT 100 GOALS FOR THE CLUB SINCE MARK HATELEY IN 1994. HOW MANY OF THESE GOLDEN GOALS - 31 IN TOTAL – DO YOU REMEMBER FROM THE 2008/09 CAMPAIGN?

1 goal – Rangers 2 Hearts 0 – SPL, 16.8.08

2 goals – Rangers 2 Kilmarnock 1 – SPL, 13.9.08

1 goal – Partick Thistle 1 Rangers 2 - Co-operative Insurance Cup, 24.9.08

2 goals – Hamilton 1 Rangers 3 – SPL, 25.10.08

1 goal – Rangers 2 Hamilton 0 – Co-operative Insurance Cup, 28.10.08

3 goals – Rangers 5 Inverness CT 0 – SPL, 1.11.08

1 goal – Kilmarnock 0 Rangers 4 – SPL, 9.11.08

1 goal – Rangers 2 St Mirren 1 – SPL, 15.11.08

1 goal – Rangers 2 Aberdeen 0 – SPL, 22.11.08

3 goals – Rangers 7 Hamilton 1 – SPL, 6.12.08

1 goal – Dundee United 2 Rangers 2 – SPL, 13.12.08

1 goal – Rangers 1 Hibernian 0 – SPL, 20.12.08

2 goals – Inverness CT 0 Rangers 3 – SPL, 4.1.09

2 goals – Rangers 3 Falkirk 1 – SPL, 17.1.09

1 goal – Rangers 3 Falkirk 0 - Co-operative Insurance Cup, 27.1.09

1 goal – Rangers 3 Kilmarnock 1 – SPL, 21.2.09

1 goal – Falkirk 0 Rangers 1 – SPL, 5.4.09

1 goal – St Mirren 1 Rangers 2 – SPL, 8.4.09

2 goals – Rangers 3 Motherwell 1 – SPL, 11.4.09

1 goal – Rangers 3 St Mirren 0 – Homecoming Scottish Cup, 25.4.09

1 goal – Rangers 2 Hearts 0 – SPL, 3.5.09

1 goal – Dundee United 0 Rangers 3 – SPL, 24.5.09

RANGERS ANNUAL PLAYER OF THE YEAR

DAVID WEIR

When Walter Smith returned as Manager of Rangers in January 2007, one of his first signings was the vastly experienced defender David Weir. Last season, the veteran (he celebrated his 39th birthday in May 2009) made more first team appearances than any other Rangers player – a total of 47 starts for Smith's side. Crucially, on the road to league and cup glory, a Rangers defence quite superbly marshalled by Weir conceded only two goals in the last seven games of the 2008/09 campaign.

In early April 2009, the player was appointed Captain of the team, bringing an air of quiet authority and dignity to the position. He is, without doubt, the perfect role model both on and off the park. Speaking about Weir after last season's Homecoming Scottish Cup final, fellow defender Steven Whittaker said, 'he just keeps producing. He is unbelievable and a great professional to have around the dressing room. He's well liked and a leader. When big Davie says something everyone listens. He has that aura about him.'

Regardless of his partner in central defence (the impressive Bougherra mainly, although McCulloch and Dailly also filled in at various times), Weir stood tall week-in, week-out and had an outstanding 2008/09 campaign. Few would disagree that despite his advancing years, he is still better than many central defenders – his reading of the game and positional sense is exceptional. On the last day of the season in the baking heat of Hampden, his work rate was that of a far younger player. Despite the extreme conditions, it was a cool commanding display. His two goals last term (both headers) were scored away from home – the first at Pittodrie against Aberdeen in the 1-1 draw and the second at Rugby Park when Rangers cruised to a 4-0 win over Jim Jefferies' Ayrshire outfit.

David Weir's pride was as obvious as the smile on his face when he lifted the SPL trophy at Tannadice. Just six days later, that sense of quiet satisfaction was once again on view as he hoisted high the Homecoming Scottish Cup at Hampden after victory over Falkirk.

It had been a truly memorable campaign for both the player and the Club he has always supported.

RANGERS YOUNG SUPPORTERS

Join Rangers Young Supporters Club and get closer to all the action at Ibrox! Rangers Young Supporters is an exclusive members only club for Rangers fans aged 16 and under. Being a member is the only way to become a matchday mascot, plus when you join you receive a fantastic membership pack which includes:

MEMBERSHIP PACK

- Rangers beanie hat
- Fully loaded USB wristband containing exclusive screensavers, wallpapers and quizzes
- Rangers sports band
- Membership card
- Official certificate
- Birthday card
- 24 page newsletter 3 times a year

Plus, being a member of Rangers Young Supporters Club you are entitled to exclusive benefits including:

MEMBERSHIP BENEFITS

- The chance to be a matchday mascot
- FREE entry to SPL matches with a full paying adult [1]
- 5% discount in JJB stores [2]
- FREE entry to The Ibrox Tour with a full paying adult [3]
- The chance to be selected to take part in exclusive first-team events
- Discounts at a range of fun venues in Glasgow!

Join today, sign up for just £9.99 for juvenile season ticket holders, £15 for UK and £20 for overseas membership!

CALL 0871 702 1972^, VISIT RANGERS.CO.UK, RANGERS TICKET CENTRE OR A JJB RANGERS STORE* TO SIGN UP NOW!

Rangers Young Supporters: 0871 702 1972^
Email: broxi@rangers.co.uk
Visit: www.rangers.co.uk

[1]Games selected by the Club, call the hotline for more information. [2]Discount valid in JJB Rangers stores and JJB stores for Rangers products only. Offer excludes sale items. Only on production of a valid membership card. [3]Excluding school holidays. One tour per member, bookings must be made in advance via the hotline only. ^Calls cost 10ppm from a BT landline, mobile and other providers' charges may vary. *£9.99 season ticket holder price not available from JJB Rangers stores.

WHERE'S BROXI ???